48 LAWS OF NOW POWER

ASSOCIATED INDIVIDUALITY

KYLIE SHINE

48 Laws Of Now Power
Copyright © 2023 by Kylie Shine

All rights reserved. No part of this publication may be reproduced, distributed, or transmitted in any form or by any means, including photocopying, recording, or other electronic or mechanical methods, without the prior written permission of the author, except in the case of brief quotations embodied in critical reviews and certain other non-commercial uses permitted by copyright law.

Tellwell Talent
www.tellwell.ca

ISBN
978-0-2288-8991-5 (Hardcover)
978-0-2288-8990-8 (Paperback)
978-0-2288-8992-2 (eBook)

TABLE OF CONTENTS

Welcome v
Chapter Guide vii

SECTION 1 – ABOUT YOU

15 - Its Always About You 3
18 - Your Own Best Friend 4
38 - Let Yourself Shine 5
 3 - Positive Intentions.. 6
 5 - Personal Success... 7
34 - Becoming You... 8
 6 - Personal Light 9
22 - Power In Surrendering 10
45 - Mastering Momentum 11
28 - Creating Success 12
11 - Independent Power... 13
 1 - Always Outshine You.. 14
26 - Regret-Free Living 15
31 - Expanding Beyond.. 17

SECTION 2 – ABOUT OTHERS

39 - Valuing Contrast... 21
16 - Being Genuine With Others 22
 2 - Internal Enemies... 23
33 - Focusing On Others 24
19 - Acknowledging Others' Light 25
10 - Attracting Others.. 26
21 - Playing Games 27

37 - Storytelling Art 28
24 - Earning Respect 29
12 - Killing With Kindness 30
43 - Meaningful Connections 31
13 - Trifecta Wins 32
 7 - Value Of Teamwork 33

SECTION 3 – ABOUT LIFE

17 - The Unfolding Path 37
20 - Commit To Yourself First 38
36 - Drop The Stick 39
 4 - Power Of Words 40
 9 - Walking Your Talk 41
32 - Lure Of The Snake 42
46 - Perfect Source 43
42 - Rolling Momentum 44
35 - Timing Is Alignment 45
40 - Creating Wealth 47
30 - Expect Greatness 48
 8 - Influential Power 49
23 - Opening Your Channels 50
29 - The Vortex 51
27 - Magnetic Attraction 52
14 - Reading Vibration 53
25 - Creating The Creator 54
41 - Letting Masters In 55
44 - Reflection Identification 56
48 - Become Consciousness 57
47 - There Is No End 58

About the Author 59

WELCOME TO *48 LAWS OF NOW POWER*

Thank you for choosing this handbook. It is my hope that you will get insight from it that will help you understand your personal existence in this life. I also hope that the information in this publication will guide you toward paving a magnificent life for yourself going forward, and perhaps will help your loved ones as well.

The inspiration for this handbook came from the book, *The 48 Laws of Power*, written by American author Robert Greene. This controversial, best-selling book describes the 'laws' people today, and throughout history, have used to get and maintain power, and features manipulation as a key.

Upon reading Greene's book, the idea of manipulation did not resonate with me, so I've written this handbook to convey the idea that the power comes from oneself.

Drawing on the insight of Abraham Hicks, bestselling American author of *The Law of Attraction*, I have created a set of basic laws to empower each and every one of us to achieve desires through internally creative means rather than by using others. I have also been influenced by *The Power of Now: A Guide to Spiritual Enlightenment*, by Eckhart Tolle.

I hope you enjoy reading *48 Laws of Now Power*.

Kylie Shine

CHAPTER GUIDE

This handbook corresponds chapter for chapter with Robert Greene's book. I have rewritten the chapters using his concepts but focusing on personal power rather than manipulation power.

There are three sections in this book:

- About You
- About Others
- About Life

The chapters in these sections appear to be in random order because each chapter from the Greene book aligns with one of these sections according to topic rather than numeric value.

SECTION 1

ABOUT YOU

15

ITS ALWAYS ABOUT YOU

Real satisfaction comes from acknowledging and understanding that you are the only person you need to be concerned about; in fact, you cannot really be of value to others until you are of value to yourself.

Some people hold a false belief that you should not matter as much to yourself as others do. We are encouraged to put the needs and wants of others ahead of our own desires. Putting attention on others disconnects us from our position of personal power.

One way to stay focused on yourself is to identify how things are turning out for you in any moment; if they are going well, then you can surmise that you are in tune with yourself. If they're not, it's likely you're out of tune and focused on something other than your own well-being and satisfaction.

18

YOUR OWN BEST FRIEND

Real satisfaction comes from being comfortable in the silence of your own company and knowing you don't need anyone else to be happy.

Some people hold a false belief that if we are not in the company of others, loneliness will result; however, learning about ourselves helps us learn about others and so the happier you are in your own company, the more interesting it becomes when you seek happiness with others. If we are not happy with ourselves, the consequence is that we end up running from ourselves, whether we realise it or not.

One way to be your own best friend is, when faced with decisions, to ask yourself, 'What would I like?' and wait for a mental and emotional response before creating an action/solution. If you keep doing this, you will start connecting with your instincts more and more.

38

LET YOURSELF SHINE

Real satisfaction comes from loving yourself enough to understand the radiance you can create. This radiance starts from the inside and expands out into your physical world, affecting everything.

Some people hold a false belief that we must contain our radiance and stay at a similar—often lower—level as those around us. This does not allow us to be fully comfortable expressing ourselves. A consequence of this is that we limit ourselves, putting roadblocks in the way of fully owning our own existence. When we remove these roadblocks, we flourish, gain positive momentum and learn to fully enjoy our own existence as well as the existence of others.

One way to let yourself shine is to really focus on how you're interacting with others. Be present and engaging and see if you're letting yourself flow or putting blockers up. If you are putting blockers up, it may be a way to subconsciously keep yourself line yourself up others who are not as happy and flowing as you are.

3

POSITIVE INTENTIONS

Real satisfaction comes from feeling satisfied and in tune with your intentions, thoughts and desires and knowing that you are creating well-being both in and around yourself.

Some people hold a false belief that you can trick people into thinking your intentions are different from your true desires. For example, your intention might be to have a particular person join you for lunch, but your desire might be to have that person see your for your true self and love you. A consequence might be that, by not acknowledging your desire, you will not achieve it or move forward.

Align your positive intentions and your desires by monitoring your decision-making. Make an intention to think a second before acting. Use that time to ask yourself, 'Will I later regret this?' and see if you change your decision. If you have changed your mind, rethink the situation so that you can create desirable outcomes.

5

PERSONAL SUCCESS

Real satisfaction at personal success is twofold. First, it comes from the empowerment generated by achieving outcomes you envisioned. Second, since no outcome can be completely predetermined, it comes from enjoying the journey along the way. Ultimately, personal achievement is knowing that you can be independent and look after yourself.

Some people hold a false belief that success can only be measured financially, or that it is something only smart people achieve. This is false because there are limitless definitions of success. To one person, losing ten pounds is success. To another, creating a multinational corporation is success. What all success has in common is that it requires focused attention and belief in your own power to achieve it. If you do not have these things, you will struggle and never experience success of your own.

One way to create personal success is to identify an ideal outcome, or goal, and start working toward it. Start with something achievable, like learning twenty words in sign language. Setting clear boundaries around what success looks like will give you the best chance of achieving success.

34

BECOMING YOU

Real satisfaction comes from knowing that you are who you are meant to be; being excited at the continual becoming of you; and, enjoying the unfolding of a life that is just as you dreamed it would be.

Some people hold a false belief that we aren't in full control of our lives; that too many external factors keep us apart from ourselves; and that others are to blame for our situations. A consequence of this false belief is thinking we are owed things, and are victims of other people's greed. This creates a mindset of poverty and lack, which can cause us to miss out on all the magical moments that line up each day for every one of us.

One way to continually move into 'becoming you' is to change your focus. Realise that the hardships you've experienced are not the biggest influence in your life. Instead, celebrate your successes. Shift your focus onto bettering yourself every day, and you will be surprised by the changes that will occur in your life.

6

PERSONAL LIGHT

Real satisfaction comes from being able to feel the wholeness of who you are, and to bask in your own glow whilst fully experiencing this world we live in.

Some people hold a false belief that people who shine bright are magnets for negative emotions from others. This belief can cause some people to 'shade over' aspects of themselves, either because they are afraid of wounding others with their brilliance, or because they are afraid of getting emotionally hurt by negative feedback. Self-dimming is counter-productive. Whether we dim ourselves or not, we have no control over how others perceive us; however, we are not being true to ourselves if we don't allow our personal lights to shine.

One way to keep your personal light shining is to be mindful of your own moods. When you catch yourself slipping from a sunny mood into a cloudy one, catch this transition and commit to moving back into a better one. Keep your light shining and healthy and it will help you manifest positive energy.

22

POWER IN SURRENDERING

Real satisfaction comes from knowing when to relax into the flow of life and stop futilely resisting it.

Some people hold a false belief that we must be right, or win, when interacting with others. This is a victor/victim perception that doesn't promote common goals or understanding in the greater community. When we live our lives ready for a fight, and need to continually justify our positions on things, the only victims are ourselves. All fights are an internal battle first. The best approach to dialogue, or other social interaction, is to direct our focus into the ease and flow of surrender. This shifts personal power into the moment, allowing us to be present and enjoy a positive outcome.

The next time you're in situation where confrontation is present, ask yourself, 'What would happen if I surrendered now?' and then let go of antagonistic feelings and enjoy freedom. With practice, this will become a great empowerment experience that will allow you to reconnect with yourself.

45

MASTERING MOMENTUM

Real satisfaction comes from being able master your momentum as you keep rolling forward with all your decisions and choices. Ideally, you should be able to relax as much as you like or boost yourself as much as you like once you've got full forward movement. How fast you roll depends on you and how ready you are to keep rolling.

Some people hold a false belief that increasing momentum will cause loss of control, but momentum is not instant; it is a force that builds, so there is time to adjust. Trying to suppress momentum out of fear will hold you back from enjoyable moments that could advance you into more of whatever you want, though there are tipping points in both directions. Too much momentum can lead to excess and unbalance (manic impulse); too little can lead to lack and unbalance (depressive impulse). Find a stable speed so you can enjoy the ride.

One way to master the speed of your momentum is to choose something relatively easy for you, such as writing a short story, and see how long you can focus on the task, and how far you can follow without forcing it during the course of a week. When the week is up, assess your experience using interest and pleasure as barometers.

28

CREATING SUCCESS

Real satisfaction comes from being bold enough to create your own success in your life and, by doing so, enhance the ability others to do so as well.

Some people hold a false belief that successful people are just lucky, and they've inherited or been given their success rather than earning it themselves. An extension of this false belief is that we don't have the same opportunities to create our *own* success and are therefore lacking. Success, however, comes in many forms. Identifying success as it applies to your own life is the key to building subsequent success.

One way to continue creating success is to pick something about your daily life that you would like to build upon—for example increasing the amount of weight you can lift at the health club or making three new friends—and then set a time limit for achieving it. Work on it bit by bit until you achieve success.

11

INDEPENDENT POWER

Real satisfaction comes from being able to provide for yourself, sustaining your own life and even the lives of others if you desire to do so.

Some people hold a false belief that power is an external force we have little control over, and that other people are in control our personal power, or ability to shine. This is flawed because every individual has personal power. They key is recognizing it and learning to access it. If you negate your own power, you never fully connect to your own internal power source, which is one of the greatest gifts of life.

One way to get independent power is to align yourself to the consciousness of your existence using pathways that resonate for you. These pathways could be mediation, prayer, being in nature or any other activity that brings you into the moment. Accessing this level of consciousness will help you create forward momentum and generate a flow that will lead you into feelings of ease, satisfaction and calmness.

1

ALWAYS OUTSHINE YOU

Real satisfaction comes from personal achievement.

Some people hold a false belief that other people have a greater right to happiness and success than they do, and that they don't deserve that same happiness.

A consequence of this false belief is a tendency to hold oneself down, and never reach toward life up in the sunshine, which is a better experience. Being able to listen to ourselves, and trust our own judgement, is the starting point for becoming more aware of possibilities. In this way you can learn to 'outshine' yourself.

One way to outshine yourself is to set an intention to do something that will enhance your life, and then see it through. Start small, such as setting an intention to ring your family every week and then following through. Build on it after a week by adding another intention, or perhaps even two or three of them. See where it takes you!

26

REGRET-FREE LIVING

Real satisfaction comes from having no skeletons in your closet and no emotional ties to events from your past lived experiences.

Some people hold a false belief that we can go about our lives not caring about the negative impact our words and actions may have on ourselves and other people. Being able to make conscious decisions is the key to being able to live with forward momentum rather than carrying chains that pull you back into the past. Too often, people divide their thoughts and intentions between what happened in the past and what they wish for their future and, with the past activated in this way, it remains alive and stops people from moving forward. To be able to focus on the 'here and now'—and feel comfortable that nothing from your past is going to bite you—gives us the freedom to make good decisions based on what is relevant *now* and creates deep satisfaction.

One way to live regret-free is to monitor your words and actions. If you notice that they sometimes have negative impacts on others, then make a choice to change one your behaviour and then make efforts to stick to that decision. For example, if you are habitually rude to people in the service industry, make a point to always say, 'Thank you'; or, if you have been neglecting your health, commit to a specific time to focus on it each day. Such commitment creates new standards which will allow you to live regret free.

31

EXPANDING BEYOND

Real satisfaction comes from knowing that we are more than just physical bodies, and that we have full control of our own life path. We can influence what will manifest for us in the coming days, weeks and months.

Some people hold a false belief that their suffering is uncontrollable, and even deserved, and that that the trials and tribulations of life are how it's always going to be. This is correct in that trials and tribulations remain, but the more we learn to focus on personal growth, the more we move into new and better personal experiences. It is a personal decision to get out of negative loops and free the mind; no one can do it for you. The trick is to focus *beyond* where you are now and imagine a more desirable future.

A way to test whether you're expanding beyond your current state is to examine some qualities about yourself you'd like to change, or desires you hold, and focus on realizing those things *now*. Connect fully to, and envision, the reality you will experience when these things are realised. Bask in this feeling as long as you can and know that it's as true when you are envisioning it as it will be when it manifests.

SECTION 2

ABOUT OTHERS

39

VALUING CONTRAST

Real satisfaction comes from fully appreciating that everything that is happening in your life is happening because you dreamed it into creation.

Some people hold a false belief that bad events happen after something good, creating a push/pull dynamic that impedes forward momentum. But conflict does not always impede momentum. Sometimes it spurs it by providing contrast. When conflict occurs, allow it to pass without becoming personally and emotionally involved. Then examine the contrast. This will help you more effectively decide what you value most in any given situation.

One way to know you're valuing contrast is, when you're in an emotional situation, to observe what is going on and try to determine what message is in it for you. This is a good way to move through traumatic events. It will help you to find the good, even in the darkest moments.

16

BEING GENUINE WITH OTHERS

Real satisfaction comes from being comfortable being yourself, which allows you to express yourself from the heart and be genuine with others in what you say and do.

Some people hold a false belief that other people's power is greater than their own, which inhibits true expression and makes them respond in less than genuine ways. Sensitive, perceptive people can see through ungenuine people because with the ungenuine, words and actions often do not align. If you struggle with being genuine, learn to trust your own personal power so that you can engage in more meaningful ways with others and not miss out on personal expansion and the warmth that comes from caring about others.

One way to be gauge your ability to be genuine with others is to notice how present you are in social interactions. Do you listen as much as you speak?

2

INTERNAL ENEMIES

Real satisfaction comes from being your own best friend.

Some people hold a false belief that other people are responsible for their failings and lack of traction in moving forward. This makes them blame others for their failures, but the truth is that personal growth is an internal progression and has nothing to do with anyone else. Let go of blame and regret; events that happened in the past aren't happening now. Keeping limiting memories alive suppresses your own ability to progress freely through life. No one owes anyone anything—but you owe it to yourself to stop listening to the stories in your mind and start listening to your true self.

A way to quell your internal enemies is to acknowledge that everyone on this Earth, including you, can only control their own actions, words, and responses. We cannot control others; we can only control how we process what other teach us. You have the choice to be either enemy or friend to yourself. Choose wisely.

33

FOCUSING ON OTHERS

Real satisfaction comes from not allowing yourself to become the victim of your own or other people's actions or stories.

Some people hold a false belief that others are the cause of their hurt and distress, that people's perceived negative actions or words are intentional and generated to create a wound. The truth is that other people have no control over how you feel. Whether their intentions are negative or not, *your* perception and internalization is what damages *you*. Focus only on your own vibration to expose how you are feeling about yourself, and the controlling nature of others will have no power over you.

Stress can cause negative mind cycles that are focused on others. One way not to get stuck focusing on others and the distractions that come from this, is to acknowledge that everyone else has their own desires and agendas, and that what suits them may not suit you. From this place, proceed with your own agenda in a mindful way. Trust in your own personal power and do not concern yourself overly with stories that come from outside yourself.

19

ACKNOWLEDGING OTHERS' LIGHT

Real satisfaction comes from seeing a sparkle in someone, responding to this true spirit inside of them, and interacting in a way that lifts you both.

Some people hold a false belief that people interact on a surface level only, and therefore whatever is expressed should be taken at face value only. This false belief shuts us off from expansive opportunities by not allowing us to really see and process soul messages from others. Such messages convey meaningful information that can guide us, and those we interact with, into personal expansion. Personal expansion is necessary to avoid repeating cycles of emotion that keep us from moving forward.

A way to connect to the light in others is to incorporate something they care about into your discussions to stimulate their passion about it. When you bring out the passion in another, you interact at a higher frequency that allows you to truly 'see' each other. Your bright spirit will bring theirs forward, and vice versa. The light that we reflect is the light we see in others.

10

ATTRACTING OTHERS

Real satisfaction comes from 'whole connectedness'—being in touch with your own mind, body, and spirit—and then meeting and interacting with others who are *also* wholly connected with themselves.

Some people hold a false belief that other people have influence over them and that they are restricted from achieving desired life outcomes because they are somehow not whole. A consequence of this false belief is that it causes us to disconnect from our instincts and allow the opinions of others to affect us. If you put your own instincts first, connecting your body, mind, and spirit in wholeness, you will create opportunities to achieve what you desire. This will attract people into your life who will guide and assist you into becoming the person you've dreamed of becoming.

One way to identify whether you're attracting positive people who will be guides on your journey is that it feels good when you are around them. When people start to annoy you it's a sign that you've lost your connection with both them and yourself. The level of person you attract reflects what attracts you to them; you can attract who and what you want, but you have to be connected to yourself first.

21

PLAYING GAMES

Real satisfaction comes from playing the game the game of life well, not from the outcome, for it is during the playing that true soul growth occurs. Games of one-upmanship played with other people are often not positively focused. This kind of game greatly stalls personal progress.

Some people hold a false belief that, during social interactions, there must be an element of trickery or dominance over another person and that there always has to be a winner and loser. A consequence of this false belief is that a positive outcome is unachievable when the negotiating parties are at odds.

One way to create a winning outcome when negotiating, or 'playing' with others is to determine desired outcomes for each party right from the start and, through the process of negotiation, work together to achieve those outcomes. Life is only a competitive game if you choose to be a competitive person.

37

STORYTELLING ART

Real satisfaction comes from sharing life experiences that surprise and delight both you and your chosen audience, and the shared enjoyment that comes from storytelling.

Some people hold a false belief that we must lie, tell mistruths, or otherwise exaggerate to connect with other people. For some, the truth is not enough. An outcome of this way of being is that people sense when we tell stories that have not been genuinely lived, and they feel manipulated in a way that's unsettling, which creates mistrust.

One way to be an effective storyteller is to use words in a creative way to keep the story interesting, but maintain an emphasis on truth. The element of truth allows others to connect more meaningfully with your words.

24

EARNING RESPECT

Real satisfaction comes from the joy that you see in others when they trust you enough to be their genuine selves around you and interact with you in a positive way.

Some people hold a false belief that they deserve unearned respect, or that others must show respect first before they return it in kind. This is backwards thinking; you receive respect when you give it to others first. Those who do not give respect to others come across as entitled and rude. Such people do not connect well with others and miss out on opportunities to advance their own experience and learning.

One way to earn respect is to listen to other people with genuine interest and, when it is your turn to speak, respond in a nonjudgmental way. This builds trust and is the foundation for true connection with others.

12

KILLING WITH KINDNESS

Real satisfaction comes from being as gracious giving gifts from your heart, such as knowledge, love and understanding, as you are receiving them. There is no way to 'kill someone with kindness' if you are sincere in your words and actions.

Some people hold a false belief that being too kind means being taken advantage of, and so they withhold their natural human instinct to share. Withholding in this way separates us from our true, giving natures which harms us more than it harms whoever we are withholding *from*. Other people overshare, or 'kill with kindness' as a way to disempower others and get the upper hand in a social situation.

A way to avoid 'killing with kindness' (understanding when your kindness isn't of interest to others) is to monitor your reason for being so generous and reign in your behaviour if you find it to be self-serving. A way to avoid being killed with kindness is to monitor the motivations of others.

43

MEANINGFUL CONNECTIONS

Real satisfaction comes from being in touch with your true self and your personal sense of power and then connecting with others who are also fully comfortable in their own power.

Some people hold a false belief that we must have power over others to lift ourselves up to a higher state of being. This is hierarchical thinking, and it doesn't have any relation to the soul's journey. We are all on individual paths and are individually capable of achieving our desires through our own focus and intentions. The progress of others is not a reflection of our own progress; to believe otherwise will simply leave you scrambling to better yourself by using others to do it.

One way to create meaningful connections is to create a positive, expansive internal state within yourself and then be open to acknowledging that in other people. Learn to genuinely respect other's choices in life, whether you would choose them or not. Applaud all successes, including your own.

13

TRIFECTA WINS

Real satisfaction comes from knowing that *everyone* wins when equitable discourse based on mutual respect is achieved.

Some people hold a false belief that 'winning' during social interactions allows them to get what they want, creating winners and losers. This is a false belief because there can be multiple winners, and there need not be losers at all, in the ideal trifecta of social interaction, which is:

1. Focused energy of more than one person is greater than the power of an individual.
2. A shared vision creates momentum that is far beyond what one can achieve alone.
3. Shared satisfactory results build community and relationships for the common good.

One way to encourage this type of trifecta is to acknowledge the diverse skills and abilities of those you are interacting with; find commonalities while in pursuit of a common goal; and celebrate achievement as a group.

7

VALUE OF TEAMWORK

Real satisfaction comes from continued, unlimited success for everyone participating in a team situation.

Some people hold a false belief that you can use people to attain success without reciprocating with your own time or resources; however, teamwork, by its nature, is about achieving success for everyone on the team. Building a team is akin to building a family; to work effectively on a team, teammates must respect one another, appreciate each person individually and genuinely want their teammates to have a great life. In return, *you* will get a great life. Nurturing relationships with teammates is the best waly to achieve continued mutual success.

One way to test the value of teamwork is to play team sports. On sports teams, the connectedness and enjoyment of the game is a direct outcome of joint participation fueled by equitability. Playing a sport will help you understand the dynamics of a properly functioning team.

SECTION 3

ABOUT LIFE

17

THE UNFOLDING PATH

Real satisfaction comes from experiencing your life unfolding in a way you anticipated and knowing it's because you created the pathways required to make it the one you dreamed of.

Some people hold a false belief that life is a dead end, that we are born, we live, we die and that we have no control over the things that happen in between. Sadly, this restrictive belief keeps many people away from the true experience of life, and they spend their lives fearing death and worrying that their time is limited. If they understood the energy within them, they would understand that time and space are infinite, and so is their energy. There is ample time to achieve all desires, as our soul's journey is infinite.

One way to enjoy the unfolding path is to practice living it. First, acknowledge your dreams and desires. Next, take a moment to feel what it would feel like to live the way you want to live and keep practicing that. By constantly visualizing in this way, you can create the unfolding path you dream about and get all you want.

20

COMMIT TO YOURSELF FIRST

Real satisfaction comes from the pure joy of living a life where you feel in full control of your journey and are enjoying the outcomes along the way.

Some people hold a false belief that they must commit to another person to be happy, but if you aren't committed to yourself first, partnership with another will become co-dependency. By expecting others to make us happy, we miss out on becoming master creators of our own reality. We cannot get what we need from others because, if they desire an expansive life, they will put themselves first.

A way to continually commit to yourself is to listen to yourself more and be discerning about whether what you hear will help you expand or contract, and then commit to expansion because that is the ultimate outcome of all life. Contraction just slows it down.

36

DROP THE STICK

Real satisfaction comes from knowing you can change your focus in an instant because you've got full control of the pathway ahead.

Some people hold a false belief that past, painful experiences are holding them back, and yet the only reason painful events thrive in a person's mind is because of a continued focus on them. Unfortunately, when you focus on something that's not enjoyable, you miss the chance to shift yourself away from it.

If you can imagine each chapter in your life as a stick, with the two ends representing extreme emotions, positive and negative, then you can also imagine just dropping that stick to focus on something else if those emotions aren't helpful.

Identify the right time to drop the stick, Each stick stays where you dropped it, so you can pick it up again when you are better prepared to carry it.

4

POWER OF WORDS

Real satisfaction comes from having an infinite number of ways to tell wonderful stories. Power lies in choosing words that match your intentions. and then delivering them in situations where your advancement is guaranteed because of your alignment.

Some people have a false belief that words don't affect people, but words can both harm and heal. It's the intention behind words that matters most. Feeling the power of intention can create a physical response, positive or negative, within both the speaker and the person receiving the words. Be aware not only of the words you speak, but the intention behind them.

One way to ensure you are using words appropriately is to gauge the emotion you are carrying behind a set of words. If you say, 'Oh, wonderful,' to a child who has handed you a drawing, you are being appreciative. If you say it to a teenager who has spilled a soft drink in the car, you are being sarcastic. One person will feel a compliment, and one will feel criticism. Your own personal growth is tied to positive intention.

9

WALKING YOUR TALK

Real satisfaction comes from being bold enough to do what you say you will do. When you are mindful of saying what you mean, and meaning what you say, you minimise your chance of overpromising and underdelivering.

Some people hold a false belief that it doesn't matter what they say, and that follow-through is not important. This type of behaviour shows disrespect toward others, and the consequence is that others will disrespect you in turn. People expect others to follow through on stated intent and sometimes look forward to the anticipated action. You honour both yourself and others by walking your talk. If you have no intention of doing what you say you're going to do, then don't say it in the first place.

One way to start walking your talk is to be mindful when you make commitments. If it is not something you really intend to honour, then don't commit to it. It's better in the long run to say, 'No, thank you,' than to say, 'Yes, please,' and not follow through.

32

LURE OF THE SNAKE

Real satisfaction comes from identifying the intentions of another person as quickly as possible so you have time to choose how you will interact with them, and how to keep yourself in your own power while doing so.

Some people hold a false belief that, to get others to do what you want, you must be manipulative. A consequence of this false belief is that you end up in the 'snake pit' using negative communication rather than positive influence. It is much more progressive and rewarding to influence people in a positive manner, and it creates satisfying, forward moving experiences. Conversely, manipulation leaves you on high alert for retaliation from those you have manipulated.

A way to be aware of the 'lure of the snake' is to check how aligned you are with yourself (what your intentions are and how honest you are being) when interacting with others. If what you are doing feels insincere, then your instincts are signaling to you to change your approach.

46

PERFECT SOURCE

Real satisfaction comes from feeling pure, positive energy flow to, through and from your body and being fully, consciously aware that it comes from the perfect source, which is the divine vibration that flows through our souls.

Some people hold a false belief that our own decisions to read, listen to or watch any variety of media, or listen to a friend or relative's negative views on something, does not affect us, but our bodies and minds are connected and so we must feed the mind with goodness if we want our bodies to support us. This also applies to self-talk. We can choose to turn off negative messaging and tune in to the perfect source if we choose to.

One way to access the perfect source is to be quiet and listen to nothing (meditate). The conscious mind is limited to what you put in it, while the unconscious mind is ever developing and is connected to the intangible perfect source. Become discerning about the vibration of the information you let into your life and listen to yourself so that you more easily manifest everything you need and want.

42

ROLLING MOMENTUM

Real satisfaction comes from continuously getting what you want while expanding yourself along the way.

Some people hold a false belief that you must have a certain checklist completed before you get to see the outcomes you desire, but the truth is that if each step along the way lines up with where you're at now, momentum toward your goal will not only build but will *compound* and will get you to your desired goal much faster. Do not succumb to the idea that your goals will take too long to achieve; instead, enjoy the milestones along the way and remember that the outcome is just the end result.

One way to get momentum rolling is to set an intention at the start of each day and to keep reminding yourself of what your focus for today is. Try this and see what starts rolling into your experiences.

35

TIMING IS ALIGNMENT

Real satisfaction comes from the alignment within yourself. When you are at one with yourself, you are in the moment and timing of your life events is in perfect harmony with your own life as it plays out.

Some people hold a false belief that time is limited, and that there is a scarcity of it. This belief causes pressure that creates stress and anxiety, leading to decisions that aren't timed properly to be in one's best interest. Do not fall victim to perceived external pressure that separates you from your own power; instead, do things that feel natural and enjoyable to you on the timetable dictated by your own instinct. This will enable you to maintain alignment with yourself as you move through your own life.

One way to get into alignment with time is to focus on understanding the relationship between timing and achievement. Notice your own relationship in this regard and then notice the relationships of those who have 'lucky breaks' and 'perfect timing' when it comes to critical life events. Such people have developed a relationship with themselves that has aligned their timing with their opportunities because they have tapped into a divine flow. Cultivate that flow. Slow down, show respect and kindness to your fellow humans, and allow the universe to aid you on your path.

40

CREATING WEALTH

Real satisfaction comes from being able to enjoy the life you dream of and having enough time and resources to be generous in sharing your bountiful life with others.

Some people hold a false belief that wealth means being monetarily gifted, but wealth comes in many forms and must be clearly defined by each individual in order for that person to achieve it. Wealth is not just money; wealth can be love for family, love for yourself, or love for your passions, among other things. When people hold wealth to only be monetary, they can become depressed at the idea that they can never achieve it and shut out gratitude and satisfaction they might otherwise have if they recognized other sources of wealth in their lives. Ironically, once we recognize those other forms of wealth, monetary wealth often follows.

One way to start the process of creating wealth is to select an area of your life you'd like to feel richer in, such as connection with loved ones, or creating a holiday fund, and then work on growing it. A continued focus on this type of wealth will create a divine flow that will allow monetary wealth to flow naturally.

30

EXPECT GREATNESS

Real satisfaction comes from aiming high, getting there and continually doing this until you achieve a level of mastery that is effortless.

Some people hold a false belief that 'something is better than nothing' … which is not necessarily true. Greatness is better than a mere 'something' and that is what we all should strive for. Why settle for less than you are capable of, or deserve? If you continue to settle, you will let yourself down again and again, which will distance you from your continued enjoyment of life. Challenge and chase are instinctual; it's up to each of us to enjoy the game and pursue greatness.

One way to pursue greatness is identify a passion and push yourself to pursue it, be it singing, public speaking, or learning a new language. Push your comfort boundaries. Move through the gates that are holding you back and fearlessly allow yourself to experience different facets of life without preconceived judgement.

8

INFLUENTIAL POWER

Real satisfaction comes from being your authentic self around others and having them respond to you because they truly admire the path you have chosen and want to emulate you.

Some people hold a false belief that people should want to follow them because they hold their own selves in high esteem; other people are aligned with their true selves and naturally attract such allegiance through influential power. In the first scenario, people who see themselves as higher than others miss the opportunity to naturally create fans. The second scenario is much more rewarding for both parties because it involves mutual respect. There's a line between fame and infamy; how you choose to present yourself is directly related your actions and words. If these align, you will receive adoration and enjoyment. If they do not, you will fall flat.

One way to develop influential power is to maintain a deep connection to yourself and your forward moving momentum. The example you set will naturally attract others.

23

OPENING YOUR CHANNELS

Real satisfaction comes from opening your energy channels to the universal vibration, allowing in more and more life-giving energy, and then stabilizing yourself in higher, advanced states.

Some people hold a false belief that we only experience life through physical sensation and so we have limited capacity; however, we also have great intuitive abilities that most people rarely tap. If cultivate such non-physical senses, we can experience more than we ever thought. It is a mistake to bypass the power of emotions and intuition because they are key to connecting with higher level, and more enjoyable, life experiences.

One way to practice tapping into higher channels is to take 15 quiet minutes, alone and uninterrupted, to be quiet and tune into your non-physical senses. See what appears in your experience.

29

THE VORTEX

Real satisfaction comes from knowing that if you're swirling in your vortex of dreams and desires and you pop out, you can jump back in and line yourself up once more with all you desire because you are in tune with this vortex.

Some people hold a false belief that we glide through life with no control about where we end up; however, we are constantly dreaming and desiring on conscious and unconscious levels, and these dreams and desires appear in our future experiences. Dreams and desires matter. Often, they are signals about how to custom-build our lives, and if we don't pay attention to them our lives may not go in the direction we want.

A way to start accessing this dream vortex is to focus on feeling good each and every day, and when you divert away from good feelings, to be able to reconnect at will. Being focused on your wellbeing and satisfaction will keep you moving toward all you desire.

27

MAGNETIC ATTRACTION

Real satisfaction comes from the understanding the invisible yet undeniable force that pulls all of existence together, and how this affects us. In human beings, individual polarities magnetize others in ways that either repel or attract us, just like with magnets.

Some people hold a false belief that chaos rules the universe and that everything is random. They do not recognize that polarity—opposite or contradictory tendencies, opinions, or aspects—affects everything. A consequence of this false belief is that we attract negative thoughts if we emit them; the benefit is that we attract positive thoughts if we emit them. We can physically see such magnetic forces (attraction and repulsion) at play through human body language.

One way to understand magnetic force between humans is to observe people interacting in social situations. If they stand close and speak in confidential tones, there is attraction there. If they fidget and look uninterested or bored, there is not.

14

READING VIBRATION

Real satisfaction comes from being able to fully tune into the vibrations of those around us, both physically and intuitively.

Some people hold a false belief that humans can't see or feel the vibrations that the world is made up of; however, many people can tune into the vibration of other humans in much the same way that they tune into a radio. Believing that we are limited to only seeing and feeling the world through basic senses is a mistake; just as snakes sense vibration, so can we. Friendly vibration is felt as a desire to interact in a pleasant manner with another; dangerous vibration will compel us to avoid another.

A way to explore vibration is to become aware of the emotional states of people as they interact. Are they smiling at one another? Expressing hostility or disinterest? Try to read what the interaction is and predict how the conversation or encounter will progress.

25

CREATING THE CREATOR

Real satisfaction comes from aligning with the creator and co-creating your own evolution continually—in essence, creating ourselves as creators.

Some people hold a false belief that we don't have control of our lives and will never get what we want. The feeling of isolation that comes from diminishing our own power is a void so powerful it takes lives. When we claim our own power, we get to experience the fullness of life in our five physical senses as well as with our vibrational senses. Living at this higher level allows us to be more in tune with our ability to manifest what we want and need in life.

One way to participate in your own creation is to first acknowledge the existence of a force that is greater than humans and then to align yourself with that force in a respectful partnership. Know that everything is designed to work out well and that the opportunities and choices you make are leading you on the path you are meant to be on.

41

LETTING MASTERS IN

Real satisfaction comes from consciously experiencing the creative force that is available to us all when we're in a state of flow, ease, and happiness and acknowledging that your enjoyment of this force can be enhanced by the presence of one who is further along the creative path.

Some people hold a false belief that the only way we can move forward is by demonstrating how intellectually smart we are. Unfortunately, such intellectualism creates a boundary around progress in some areas of life. Luckily some shifts in perspective can change this and make your creative force as great as you want it to be, and as expansive as you need it to be. Do not write off opportunities because you need validation for being smart; instead allow a master to identify talents in you that lie beyond the intellectual so you can become what you are meant to be.

On way to allow a master in is to do identify someone who effortlessly accesses the things you want and to emulate them. Other similar people will present themselves to you when you are ready, and then you will feel the combined power of all those masters, which will create passion and joy in your soul.

44

REFLECTION IDENTIFICATION

Real satisfaction comes from knowing that behaviour you notice in others reflects your own, either consciously or unconsciously—and that in both cases you like what you see. When you display calmness, compassion, and a well-integrated sense of self, the same will be returned to you.

Some people hold a false belief that other people evoke responses from us with their behaviour, and that it is their fault when we feel the way we do about their actions. The truth is, when we process social interactions, we sometimes frame them with negative stories from our past that create strong emotions and reflect beliefs that no longer serves us (reflection identification).

A way to identify whether reflection identification is impacting you is to note when someone's behaviour triggers a negative emotion and to identify the belief that caused you to process the behaviour as negative. Ultimately, we are responsible for our own emotional responses and if we focus on the other person instead of ourselves, we miss opportunities for personal growth.

48

BECOME CONSCIOUSNESS

Real satisfaction comes from having a sense of yourself in the context of creation.

Some people hold a false belief that we are only flesh and bone and do not acknowledge the idea of having a spirit or soul. When our level of consciousness transcends physical existence, it provides greater opportunity to create a better way forward. The benefit of recognizing the spiritual aspect of life is a greater and more enjoyable existence on this physical plane. We are an extension of greater source energy and are inextricably linked at a cellular level. We are the forward focused drivers of our own vibrational frequencies and are made to connect with other vibrational frequencies along the way.

A way to 'become consciousness' is to read this and other books that describe the interconnectedness of life and creation.

47

THERE IS NO END

Real satisfaction comes from living today, not fearing 'the end' and fully enjoying the journey of life that never ends.

Some people hold a false belief that once we die, that's the end; however, our consciousness, and the energy we are always connected to, is eternal. It flows through all, always. Physical mortality is inevitable, but energy carries on. When you understand that you are eternal, then you will release the fear of knowing your time here on Earth will end and will move through life with no resistance and no fear.

One way to know there is no end is to get there … and you never will.

ABOUT THE AUTHOR

The inspiration for this handbook came from the desire to switch from the concept of manipulation to get what you want into mastery of self to get what you want.

www.ingramcontent.com/pod-product-compliance
Lightning Source LLC
LaVergne TN
LVHW051226070526
838200LV00057B/4626